He is not here;

Poems and Prayers for Easter by Mary Fleeson

He is not here;

The man you call the Christ,
In this cold, damp place
that tells of death and sorrow.

He is not here;
The man you call Jesus,
In this repository of bones
where no Spirit dwells.

He is not here;
The man you call Messiah,
In this hopeless darkness
of dread and fear.

In my darkness,
be my light.
In my loneliness,
be my companion.
In my death,
be my salvation.

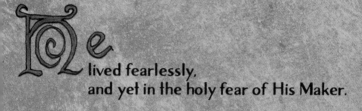

He
lived fearlessly,
and yet in the holy fear of His Maker.

He courted rebelliousness,
and yet preached peace and love.

He spoke of salvation to thousands,
and yet cared enough
to save every last one.

Help me
to fully live
in Your presence,
Help me
to fear only
Your power,
Help me
to care enough
to pray
for those who live
without Your light.

is this it?

We've all wondered.
Is this the life we're meant to live?
What have we missed?

To still feel the emptiness - hold me!

Our deepest desires calling - hear me!

Our soul crying out for home - save me!

Infinite God fill me with Your Spirit,
Hold me in Your loving arms,
Hear the prayers I cannot speak,
Save me through Your mercy.

 in the tomb

but in our darkness
He may be found.

Not within walls
but inside every place
He may be found.

Not in the forest,
beach or park
or town or city
or open space
but of course there
He may be found.

Infinite God find me in my darkness,
Let me find You within,
Let me find You without,
Let me find You in all.

here;

in this moment
I give myself to You,

My mind - amazing, creative
and wonderfully made,
yet so often distracted,
wayward and scared.
I give it to You.

My body - amazing, creative
and wonderfully made,
yet so often tired,
weak and damaged.
I give it to You.

My spirit - amazing, creative
and wonderfully made,
yet so often doubting,
needy and confined.
I give it to You.

Here; in this moment
I give myself to You.

He is Jesus,
the Christ,
My blessing.
He is Jesus,
the Messiah,
My Saviour.
He is Jesus,
the Lord,
My Encourager.
He is Jesus,
the Master,
My Teacher.
He is Jesus,
the Word,
My Life.
He is Jesus,
the Man,
My Friend.
He is Jesus,
the King,
My Protector.

Artwork Notes

He is not here; He is risen,
just as He said.

Matthew 28:6

"The Son of Man must suffer many
things and be rejected by the elders,
chief priests and teachers of the
law, and that he must be killed and
after three days rise again".

Mark 8:31

This piece includes imagery that depicts
the day of resurrection, Easter Day. In the
lower half we can see the tomb with the
stone rolled to the side. The inside of the
tomb offers a spiralling fall into the
separation from God, a dark, chaotic
journey surrounded by the crown of
thorns that represents that this was Jesus'
sacrificial journey taken on our behalf.

The rolled stone is lighter in colour and
offers hope through the knot rising and
directing us to the empty cross and the
Spirit as a dove flying freely. The leaves
and Spring colours remind us of new life.

He is not here; He is risen just as HE SAID

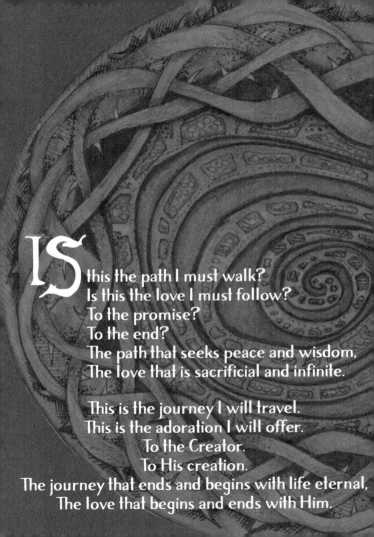

IS this the path I must walk?
Is this the love I must follow?
To the promise?
To the end?
The path that seeks peace and wisdom,
The love that is sacrificial and infinite.

This is the journey I will travel.
This is the adoration I will offer.
To the Creator.
To His creation.
The journey that ends and begins with life eternal,
The love that begins and ends with Him.

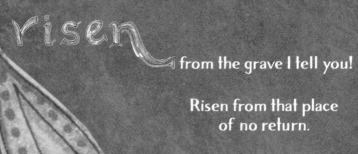

risen from the grave I tell you!

Risen from that place
of no return.

Risen from the agony
of separation.

And I pray that I will rise
to the life eternal,
holding the hand
of my Saviour.

And I pray
that I will live now,
as though the earth
were heaven.

And I pray
that I will live now,
as though the people
around me,
were You.

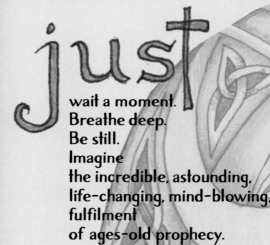

just

wait a moment.
Breathe deep.
Be still.
Imagine
the incredible, astounding,
life-changing, mind-blowing,
fulfilment
of ages-old prophecy.

Just remember.
Breathe deep.
Be still.
Understand
that you are part
of that amazing story,
His story,
is your
story.

As the flower turns its face
towards the sun
I turn to You.
As the waters cover the shore
with the incoming tide,
Protect me Lord.
As the bird flies high
gliding on the thermals,
Lift my spirit Lord.
As the vine climbs,
growing good fruit
Let me grow in You.

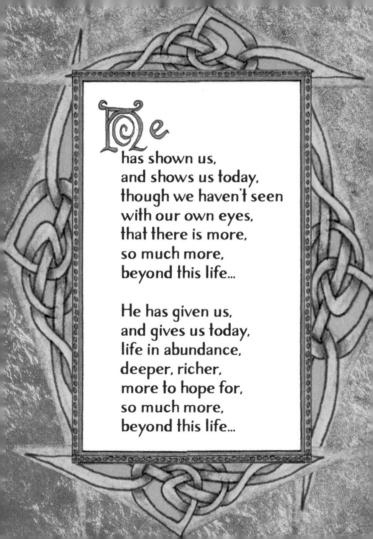

He
has shown us,
and shows us today,
though we haven't seen
with our own eyes,
that there is more,
so much more,
beyond this life...

He has given us,
and gives us today,
life in abundance,
deeper, richer,
more to hope for,
so much more,
beyond this life...

SAID

what?

That I am enough?
That my frail faith is enough?
Said what?
That I am actually
more than enough?

That the creator God
who sent His Son,
to save us,
to save me,
did it because
I am enough.

After three days, 'I will rise'.
Three days in the tomb,
Three days separated from the Father,
Three days to restore the Temple.

Take three lengths of time,
Three hours...
Three days...
More...

One to contemplate the mystery,
One to forgive yourself and others,
One to prepare your heart and mind,
for His promise.

Then rejoice!
For He is Risen,